GREAT ARCHAEOLOGICAL DISCOVERIES IN HISTORY

William of Rome

CONTENTS

GREAT ARCHAEOLOGICAL DISCOVERIES IN HISTORY

William Romani

A JOURNEY THROUGH HISTORY

Welcome to a fascinating journey through the mysterious recesses of the past, where the shadows of antiquity dissipate to reveal buried treasures and silent testimonies of forgotten civilizations. In GREAT ARCHAEOLOGICAL DISCOVERIES OF HISTORY, we will immerse ourselves in the richness of human history through the main archaeological discoveries that have transformed our understanding of the world we inhabit.

From the mysterious cave paintings of the Altamira Cave in Spain to the majestic pyramids of Egypt, each chapter of this book is a window to a distant era, to sacred places, and to civilizations that once flourished. Join us as we explore places like Stonehenge in the United Kingdom, the Temple of Karnak in Egypt, and the Valley of the Kings, where the footprints of pharaohs and nobles tell us their stories in carved hieroglyphics.

Each discovery is a puzzle that we unravel, from the construction techniques to the myths and legends that surround these sacred enclaves. How was each location discovered? What is its importance in human history? Are there myths and curses surrounding them? These questions, among others, will be explored in each chapter, giving you a deep and exciting insight into our archaeological heritage.

This book is not only a detailed account of exceptional discoveries, but also a tribute to human curiosity and the perseverance of those who have unearthed the secrets of our past. By immersing ourselves in these narratives, we discover connections between distant cultures, understand the evolution of technology and spirituality, and reflect on the richness and complexity of the human experience over time.

Join us on this archaeological journey, where each page brings us a little closer to the voices of those who, despite having faded in time, continue to whisper to us from the past. GREAT ARCHAEOLOGICAL DISCOVERIES OF HISTORY is a tribute to archaeology, a discipline that allows us to unearth the traces of our ancestors and, in doing so, better understand who we are and where we come from. Let the exploration begin!

What places will we visit in this book?

Pompeii (Italy) - 1599: Roman city preserved by the eruption of Vesuvius.

The Parthenon (Greece) - 18th century: Temple on the Acropolis of Athens.

Teotihuacan (Mexico) - 18th century: Pre-Columbian city with imposing pyramids.

Persepolis (Iran) - 18th century: Capital of the Achaemenid Empire.

Herculaneum (Italy) - 1738: Roman city buried by the eruption of Vesuvius along with Pompeii.

Carnac (France) - 1729: Set of megalithic alignments.

Palenque (Mexico) - 1773: Site of the Mayan civilization.

Chichen Itza (Mexico) - 1841: Mayan city with a prominent pyramid.

Akrotiri (Greece) - 1867: Minoan settlement on the island of Santorini.

Altamira Cave (Spain) - 1879: Cave paintings dating from the Stone Age.

Ur (Iraq) - 19th century (ancient discovery, but significant excavations in the 19th century): Important Sumerian city.

Nineveh (Iraq) - 19th century: Ancient Assyrian city.

Hattusa (Türkiye) - 19th century: Hittite capital.

Ancient Troia (Turkey) - 19th century: Ancient city associated with the Trojan War.

Urartian (Armenia) - 19th century: Ancient kingdom in the Anatolia region.

Machu Picchu (Peru) - 1911: Inca citadel in the Andes.

Mohenjo-daro (Pakistan) - 1922: City of the ancient Indus Valley civilization.

Mount Alban (Mexico) - 1931: Zapotec city in Oaxaca.

Cave of Lascaux (France) - 1940: Paleolithic cave paintings.

Qumran Caves (West Bank) - 1947: Where the Dead Sea Scrolls were found.

Catalhöyük (Türkiye) - 1958: Neolithic settlement.

possible (Syria) - 1964: Ancient city with cuneiform texts.

Göbekli Tepe (Türkiye) - 1994: Archaeological complex with Neolithic temples.

Templo de Karnak (Egypt) - Ancient: Temple complex in Luxor.

Stonehenge (United Kingdom) - Various discovery dates: Megalithic stone circle in England.

King's Valley (Egypt) - Ancient: Necropolis of Egyptian pharaohs.

POMPEYA (ITALY - 1599)

Pompeii, the city buried by time, emerges as a frozen testament to the splendor and tragedy of ancient Rome. This archaeological site, rediscovered in 1599 by the Italian architect Domenico Fontana, reveals a unique vision of daily life in the 1st century AD, preserved in the volcanic ashes of Mount Vesuvius.

A Journey in Time: The City that Eternity Forgot

Pompeii, with its cobblestone streets, richly decorated houses and magnificent theaters, offers a detailed snapshot of life in ancient Rome. From the frescoes that adorn the walls to the ruins of temples and public baths, the city provides an unparalleled perspective on the sophistication and complexity of Roman society at its peak.

Among the Ashes: The Renaissance of Pompeii

The rediscovery of Pompeii in 1599 by Domenico Fontana marks a crucial chapter in archaeological history. While carrying out canal work, Fontana stumbled upon the ruins of the buried city. Although initially believed to be Herculaneum, another site affected by the eruption, the recognition of Pompeii opened the doors to understanding

Roman life in its splendor and its tragic end.

Under the Shadow of Vesuvius: Importance of the Discovery

The discovery of Pompeii has unearthed a time capsule, providing archaeologists with an unparalleled insight into Roman life. From the luxurious atriums of the houses to the vibrant forums, Pompeii sheds light on the architecture, culture and customs of a civilization that lies beneath layers of ash. This segment explores the historical importance of Pompeii and its role in understanding antiquity.

The Echo of Disaster: Myths and Realities of Pompeii

Unlike some places, Pompeii does not carry with it myths or legends, but its discovery and study have revealed moving stories of a city that was petrified in time. This section examines the narratives surrounding Pompeii and the challenges faced by archaeologists in preserving and understanding its legacy.

Unraveling the Mysteries of Pompeii: Five Amazing Curiosities

1. The Art of Conservation: Volcanic ash, although destructive, acted as a natural preservative, preserving buildings, frescoes and objects.

2. The Vibrant Forum: The Forum of Pompeii served as the nerve center of the city, hosting commercial and political activities.

3. Theater of Everyday Life: The Grande Theater, with a capacity of 5,000 spectators, was a crucial place for entertainment and artistic expression.

4. The Mysteries of Graffiti: Inscriptions on walls offer a glimpse into everyday life, from romantic messages to commercial advertisements.

5. Petrified Victims: Human forms frozen in the position of their last actions reveal the intensity of the volcanic disaster.

THE PARTHENON (GREECE - 18TH CENTURY)

The Parthenon, a majestic architectural jewel crowning the Acropolis of Athens, stands as an enduring monument to the greatness of ancient Greece. Built in the 5th century BC. Under the supervision of the architect Phidias, this temple dedicated to the goddess Athena Parthenos has endured throughout the centuries. However, it was in the 18th century that renewed interest in this Hellenic icon was sparked.

Standing Columns: The Architectural Splendor of Greece

El Partenón, with its imposing Doric columns and meticulously carved friezes, embodies the aesthetic perfection of classical Greek architecture. Dedicated to Athena, the goddess of wisdom, just war and the arts, the temple symbolizes the cultural and political apogee of Athens during the golden siglo of Greece.

The Spark of the 18th Century: Renewed Interest in the Antique

Throughout the 18th century, the Parthenon captured the

imagination of European scholars and artists immersed in a resurgence of interest in classical antiquity. From travelers to philosophers, the Parthenon became a cultural obsession, influencing the architecture, arts and philosophy of the time.

Parthenon: Beyond the Golden Columns

The rediscovery of the Parthenon in the 18th century not only revitalized interest in ancient Greece, but also influenced the appreciation of classical architecture. Through artistic explorations and representations, the Parthenon became a symbol of the Hellenic revival, inspiring the neoclassical aesthetic that characterized European art and architecture during the century.

The Silent Ruins: Between Myths and Discoveries

Although there are no specific myths associated with the Parthenon, its rediscovery and study over the centuries have been peppered with romantic legends and challenges. Exploring the silent ruins of the Parthenon reveals stories of looting, controversy, and efforts to preserve this archaeological treasure.

Deciphering the Mysteries of the Parthenon: Five Fascinating Curiosities

1. Pentelicus Marble: The construction of the Parthenon used white marble from Pentelicus, a quarry near Athens.

2. The Caryatids of the Erechtheion: The nearby temple, Erechtheion, features caryatids, columns sculpted as female figures.

3. The Myth of the Metope: The metopes of the Parthenon represent various mythological scenes, from the Gigantomachy to the Amazons.

4. Lord Elgin and the Elgin Marbles: Lord Elgin removed sculptures from the Parthenon, known as the Elgin Marbles, which are now in the British Museum.

5. Controversial Reconstructions: Efforts to reconstruct parts of the Parthenon have generated controversies over authenticity and preservation.

TEOTIHUACÁN (MEXICO - 18TH CENTURY)

Teotihuacán, the city of the gods, lies as a mysterious archaeological site in Mexico, revealing the greatness of a pre-Columbian civilization. Although its splendor reached its peak between the 1st and 7th centuries, it was in the 18th century when this ancient city once again aroused the interest of explorers and scholars.

Pyramids to Heaven: Witnesses to the Mexica Past

Teotihuacán, with its iconic pyramids of the Sun and the Moon, is an imposing testimony of the engineering and urban planning of the Teotihuacan civilization. The city was home to a diverse population and was a cultural epicenter that influenced the surrounding regions, leaving a legacy that persists today.

Teotihuacano Rebirth: The Rediscovery of the 18th Century

Although the ruins of Teotihuacán were known to local inhabitants, it was not until the 18th century that they attracted the attention of explorers and scholars. The expeditions and the first archaeological studies of this abandoned city marked the beginning of a resurgence of interest in pre-Columbian cultures in Mexico.

Teotihuacán in the 18th Century: A Rescue from Oblivion

The rediscovery of Teotihuacán in the 18th century had a significant impact on the understanding of Mexico's pre-Columbian history. As explorers and archaeologists unraveled its secrets, the city became an enigma that intrigued the society of the time, influencing the perception and appreciation of indigenous cultures.

Guardians of the Pyramids: Myths and Challenges of Teotihuacán

Although legends and myths directly associated with Teotihuacán are scarce, the process of rediscovery and study has been accompanied by challenges and mysterious narratives. This section explores the shadows that surround Teotihuacán, from mythological interpretations to obstacles in archaeological research.

Unraveling the Enigmas of Teotihuacán: Five Fascinating Curiosities

1. The Causeway of the Dead: A main avenue that connects the pyramids of the Sun and the Moon, suggesting a cosmic connection.

2. Tepantitla Murals: Frescoes depicting divinities and rituals, offering a glimpse into everyday life.

3. The Citadel and Temple of the Feathered Serpent: A monumental complex associated with the ruling elite and

serpentine symbols.

4. The Mysterious Disappearance: Although the exact cause remains unknown, the city was abandoned in the 7th century.

5. Pyramid of the Moon and Ritual Nudity: Theories suggest rituals of nudity in the Pyramid of the Moon, linked to fertility and renewal.

PERSEPOLIS (IRAN - 18TH CENTURY)

Persepolis, the jewel of the ancient Persian Empire, stands as a testament to the grandeur and sophistication of the Achaemenid civilization. Built in the 6th century BC, this palatial city was rediscovered in the 18th century, revealing a resplendent chapter of Iranian history.

Palaces on the Hillsides: The Splendor of Persepolis

Persepolis, with its majestic palaces and colonnades, represents the opulence and architectural organization of Achaemenid Persia. The city, founded by Darius I, served as the ceremonial and administrative center of the empire, capturing the imagination with its sculpted reliefs and monumental structures.

Lights in the Hills: The Rebirth of Persepolis

Although Persepolis was never completely forgotten, its rediscovery in the 18th century marked a new era of recognition and study. European explorers, such as Antoine-Joseph Dezallier d'Argenville, brought international attention to this archaeological wonder, unraveling its buried secrets.

Persepolis Resurges: A Link to Persian Antiquity

The rediscovery of Persepolis in the 18th century revitalized interest in Iran's rich history. As studies and excavations revealed the magnificence of this ancient city, Persepolis became a symbol of the connection between Iranian modernity and its glorious past.

Guardians of the Lost City: Myth and Reality of Persepolis

Although no specific myths are associated with Persepolis, the ruins have been shrouded in mysteries and narratives. Exploring the shadows of Persepolis reveals challenges in its conservation and efforts to preserve the silhouettes carved into the stones.

Unraveling the Enigmas of Persepolis: Five Fascinating Curiosities

1. The Portal of All Nations: A majestic entrance decorated with reliefs representing tributes from the different nations of the empire.

2. Apadana Palace: An imposing audience hall where the kings received tributes and celebrated festivities.

3. Triumphal Frieze Reliefs: Sculpted scenes that illustrate the procession of delegations carrying gifts to the Persian king.

4. The Fire of Alexander: The destruction of Persepolis by the forces of Alexander the Great, a controversial and debated episode.

5. Los Tres Portales: Three colonnades on the Apadanas

Terrace, each one with a unique architectural style.

HERCULANEUM (ITALY - 1738)

Herculaneum, the city buried by the fury of Mount Vesuvius next to Pompeii, stands as an archaeological treasure that has stood the test of time. Rediscovered in 1738 by Spanish engineer Rocque Joaquín de Alcubierre, this Roman city offers a unique insight into daily life in the 1st century AD.

Beneath the Ashes: The Rise of Herculaneum

Herculaneum, located on the Bay of Naples, was a prosperous and elegant Roman city. Its luxurious villas, public baths and theater speak of the refinement of the society that inhabited it. The eruption of Vesuvius in 79 AD. He buried it in layers of ash, preserving its structures and artifacts for future generations.

The Engineer and the Forgotten City: Rocque Joaquín de Alcubierre

The rediscovery of Herculaneum in 1738 is attributed to the military engineer Rocque Joaquín de Alcubierre. During the drilling of a well in the current city of Resina, vestiges leading to ancient Herculaneum were found. This discovery triggered a series of excavations that revealed a city frozen in time.

Herculaneum Unearthed: A Window into Ancient Rome

The discovery of Herculaneum allowed archaeologists and historians to explore a well-preserved Roman city, providing a detailed insight into daily life in ancient times. Residential structures, frescoes and daily objects have shed light on the culture and customs of the inhabitants of Herculaneum.

The Ghost City: Myth and Reality of Herculaneum

While there are no specific myths or legends associated with Herculaneum, the image of the city buried by the volcanic eruption has captured the imagination and generated stories about its sudden disappearance. Meeting the challenges of conservation and excavation has been crucial to unraveling the secrets of this buried city.

Deciphering the Mysteries of Herculaneum: Five Fascinating Curiosities

1. The Villa of the Papyrus: A luxurious villa with an impressive library that housed carbonized papyrus scrolls.

2. Splendid Frescoes: Well-preserved wall paintings, depicting mythological scenes, landscapes and daily life.

3. The Antiquarian and Works of Art: Discoveries of sculptures and works of art that demonstrate the aesthetic taste of the Roman elite.

4. Herculaneum Beach: The eruption modified the coastline, leaving the old beach now inside the city.

5. Advanced Hydraulic Engineering: Channeling systems and wells that show the advanced engineering of the time.

CARNAC (FRANCE - 1729)

Carnac, the enigma of the menhirs, emerges as a mystical testimony of the prehistoric past in the region of Brittany, France. Discovered in 1729 by French scholar Jean-Baptiste Bullet, this vast set of megalithic alignments offers an intriguing puzzle about the practices and beliefs of Neolithic communities.

Guardians of Antiquity: The Menhirs of Carnac

Carnac is known for its alignments of menhirs, vertical stones erected thousands of years ago. These mysterious formations stretch for miles, presenting an astonishing glimpse into the architectural prowess and cultural symbolism of Neolithic societies in Europe.

Jean-Baptiste Bullet and the Riddle of the Standing Stones

The rediscovery of Carnac in 1729 is attributed to the French scholar Jean-Baptiste Bullet. His fascination with archeology led him to explore the region of Brittany, where he came across the mysterious menhirs. This discovery sparked interest in these megalithic structures, triggering future research and excavations.

Carnac Reveals its Neolithic Past: A Sanctuary of Meanings

The discovery of Carnac provided archaeologists a window into Neolithic practices and rituals. The carefully aligned menhirs suggest a connection to the cosmos and possibly astronomical calendars. Carnac has become a key site to understand the spirituality and ingenuity of prehistoric communities.

Mysteries among the Menhirs: Legends and Challenges of Carnac

Although specific legends associated with Carnac are few, the enigmatic presence of the menhirs has inspired stories and conjecture. Challenges in interpreting its purpose and the absence of writing leave room for speculation and the construction of narratives about its origin and meaning.

Among the Standing Stones: Five Fascinating Curiosities

1. Variety of Menhirs: Carnac is home to menhirs of different sizes and shapes, some reaching notable heights.

2. Geometric Alignments: The menhirs are arranged in straight lines and geometric patterns, suggesting careful planning.

3. The Great Broken Menhir: An ancient monolith known as the Great Broken Menhir evidences the complexity of the structures.

4. Orientation Symbolism: Some menhirs are oriented towards cardinal points and astronomical events, revealing advanced knowledge.

5. Neolithic Rituals: The precise function of the menhirs remains a mystery, but there is speculation about religious rituals and ceremonies.

PALENQUE (MEXICO - 1773)

Palenque, the Mayan jewel hidden in the Chiapas jungle, was revealed to the modern world in 1773 thanks to the exploration of the Spanish captain Antonio del Río. This archaeological site, surrounded by mystery and splendor, offers a unique window into the greatness of the Mayan civilization.

The Splendor in the Jungle: Palenque and its Mayan Grandeur

Palenque, with its majestic temples and the tomb of the iconic Pakal the Great, represents the height of classical Mayan culture. Surrounded by lush tropical jungle, this archaeological site stands out for its sophisticated architecture, hieroglyphic inscriptions and artistic expressions that narrate Mayan history and mythology.

Antonio del Río and the Revelation of a Forgotten City

In 1773, Spanish captain Antonio del Río led an expedition that would reveal the wonders of Palenque. During his exploration, he discovered the ruins of ancient structures and monuments that evidenced the greatness of a civilization lost in the jungle. Their findings contributed to the knowledge of the Mayan culture.

Palenque Resucitates: Recognizing the Mayan Heritage

The discovery of Palenque in 1773 was crucial to understanding the magnificence and complexity of the Mayan civilization. The sculptures, inscriptions, and intricate architecture provided valuable clues to aspects such as religion, governance, and Mayan cosmogony, cementing Palenque's importance in Mesoamerican history.

Stories among the Ruins: Myths and Challenges of Palenque

Although there are no specific myths associated with the discovery of Palenque, the ruins have fueled the imagination with narratives about the life and events of the Mayan civilization. Challenges such as decoding hieroglyphs and accurately interpreting Mayan history have added layers of mystery to the site.

Unraveling the Enigmas of Palenque: Five Fascinating Curiosities

1. The Temple of Inscriptions: It protects the tomb of Pakal the Great and contains the largest number of known Mayan hieroglyphs.

2. Pakal the Great: The ruler whose tomb reveals intricate sculptures and a slab that has given rise to enigmatic interpretations.

3. The Palace: An impressive structure with an observatory tower that demonstrates astronomical knowledge.

4. The Group of Crosses: A group of temples that stands out for its reliefs and crosses, important elements in the Mayan cosmogony.

5. The Ball Game: A playing field that shows the importance of the ball game in ceremonies and Mayan life.

CHICHEN ITZA
(MEXICO - 1841)

Chichén Itzá, the monumental and celestial Mayan city, was revealed to the world in 1841 thanks to the American explorer John Lloyd Stephens and the British artist Frederick Catherwood. This archaeological site, which fuses Mayan architecture with influences from other cultures, stands as an impressive testament to the ingenuity and spirituality of ancient Mesoamerica.

Heaven and Earth in Stone: Chichén Itzá and its Mayan Splendor

Chichén Itzá, with its Kukulcán pyramid, the El Caracol observatory and the Ball Court, represents the confluence of Mayan architecture with Toltec influences. This site, which flourished between the 6th and 10th centuries, is a reflection of the cultural complexity and cosmic connection of the Mayan civilization.

John Lloyd Stephens and Frederick Catherwood: Pioneers of Exploration

In 1841, the expedition led by Stephens and Catherwood resulted in the discovery and detailed documentation of Chichén Itzá. Through their stories and drawings, they brought this Mayan site to international attention, revealing the greatness of a city that lay hidden in the jungle.

Chichén Itzá Wakes Up: A Legacy of Mesoamerica

The discovery of Chichén Itzá in 1841 was a milestone that contributed significantly to the archaeological and anthropological knowledge of Mesoamerica. It revealed the fusion of architectural styles, astronomical systems and ritual practices, cementing Chichén Itzá as a crucial place in the understanding of pre-Columbian civilizations.

Narratives on the Kukulcán Staircase: Myths and Challenges of Chichén Itzá

Although there are no specific myths related to the discovery, the shadows of the pyramid and Mayan stories have generated mystical interpretations. Challenges in interpreting the precise function of certain structures and allusions to Mayan deities add layers of intrigue to the site.

Unraveling the Mysteries of Chichén Itzá: Five Fascinating Curiosities

1. Kukulcán Castle: Pyramid that acts as a solar calendar, with light and shadow phenomena at the equinoxes.

2. El Caracol: Astronomical observatory with openings that follow the movement of Venus, highlighting Mayan knowledge in astronomy.

3. The Sacred Cenote: Natural well used for rituals and sacrifices, revealing religious practices of great importance.

4. Ball Court: The playing field where ritual and sports

ceremonies were carried out, with symbolic implications.

5. The Platform of Skulls: Scene of ritual representations and probably linked to the Mayan worldview.

ALTAMIRA CAVE (SPAIN - 1879)

The Altamira Cave, located in northern Spain, stands as a prehistoric sanctuary steeped in mystery and creativity. It houses an invaluable treasure: exceptionally well-preserved cave paintings dating from the Upper Paleolithic, a unique window into the life and artistic expression of the hunter-gatherer communities that populated the region more than 20,000 years ago.

The Art that Breathes: Behind the Walls of Altamira

Altamira is made up of several interconnected rooms, each adorned with artistic representations of animals, human hands and symbolic elements. The paintings, executed with mastery and detail, offer valuable clues about the worldview and creativity of early humans. Among the most notable depictions are bison, horses and deer that seem to come to life on the cave walls. The importance of Altamira lies in its ability to transport us to the past, allowing us to glimpse the minds of our ancestors. These paintings not only reflect the technical prowess of Paleolithic artists, but also shed light on their beliefs, social interactions, and the environment around them.

They are not oxen, they are bison: The Surprising Discovery

The discovery of Altamira in 1879 by Marcelino Sanz de Sautuola and his daughter María marked a momentous milestone. As they explored the cave, young Maria, astonished, exclaimed: They are not oxen, they are bison! Although Sautuola initially faced skepticism, the authenticity of the paintings was confirmed after years of research. The revelation of these prehistoric masterpieces generated controversies and debates in the academic community of the time.

Altamira: Beyond Rock Art

The discovery of the Altamira Cave has transformed our understanding of the intellectual and creative capacity of Paleolithic societies. More than a simple repository of rock art, Altamira is a tangible testimony of the symbolic and aesthetic expression of our ancestors. This segment explores the deep historical relevance of Altamira, offering insights into the daily lives, beliefs, and spiritual connection of those who created them.

Lights and Shadows: Controversies and Challenges

Although there are no myths or curses linked to Altamira, its discovery was shrouded in controversy. The academic community of the time posed challenges to Sautuola, questioning the authenticity of the paintings. This section examines the critical moments in which the truth resisted adversity, highlighting Sautuola's tenacity in defending his discovery.

Discovering the Secrets of Altamira: Five Fascinating Curiosities

1. Brushstrokes with Breath: The artists of Altamira used the pigment blowing technique, giving the paintings exceptional details.

2. Suspended Time: The cave was closed to the public for decades to preserve the paintings, allowing for their optimal conservation.

3. Replicated Inspiration: Altamira served as inspiration for the creation of replicas, allowing visitors to experience the paintings in a more accessible way.

4. Picturesque Menagerie: Varied representations, from bison to human hands, give Altamira a unique artistic wealth.

5. Global Recognition: The Altamira Cave was declared a World Heritage Site by UNESCO in 1985, consolidating its importance worldwide.

AKROTIRI (GREECE - 1867)

Akrotiri, the Pompeii of the Aegean, emerged from the ashes of history in 1867 thanks to the archaeological excavation led by the Greek archaeologist Spyridon Marinatos. This Minoan city, buried by the eruption of the Thera volcano (Santorini) in the 17th century BC, reveals a unique snapshot of life in the Bronze Age.

City of Millennial Murmurs: Akrotiri and its Mysterious Disappearance

Akrotiri, located on the island of Santorini, flourished as a prosperous Minoan settlement in the Bronze Age. Its advanced structures, impressive frescoes and complex urban systems offer a rich vision of prehistoric society before the volcanic catastrophe that plunged it into oblivion.

Spyridon Marinatos and the Renaissance of an Ancient City

In 1867, excavation led by Spyridon Marinatos unearthed the remains of Akrotiri. The careful revelation of its streets, houses and painted wall frescoes allowed archaeologists to explore an exceptionally well-preserved Minoan city, whose sudden collapse was captured in time.

Akrotiri Resurges: A Window to the Minoan World

The discovery of Akrotiri in 1867 was essential to understanding the Minoan civilization and the commercial and cultural connections in the Aegean. Its frescoes, advanced technology and architectural layout reveal a sophisticated society, contributing significantly to the knowledge of the Bronze Age in the Mediterranean.

The Silence of Santorini: Myths and Enigmas of Akrotiri

Although there are no specific myths associated with the discovery, Akrotiri's sudden disappearance has inspired speculation about the connection to the legend of Atlantis. Challenges in interpreting the exact cause of the evacuation and the mystery behind the absence of human remains add layers of mystery.

Among the Vestiges of Ash: Five Fascinating Curiosities

1. Lilies Frescoes: Paintings depicting a variety of flowers, highlighting Minoan artistic mastery.

2. Advanced Ceramics: Akrotiri reveals refined ceramics, indicating the level of technological development of the civilization.

3. The House of Frescoes: Residence that houses some of the most outstanding and complex mural paintings.

4. Plumbing System: Evidence of advanced plumbing and channeling systems in Minoan structures.

5. The Temple of the Serpent: A sanctuary with a

representation of a snake in relief, the subject of various interpretations.

FROM (IRAQ – SIGLO XIX)

Ur, the ancient Sumerian city of wealth and splendor, was unearthed in the 19th century by British archaeologist Sir Leonard Woolley. This archaeological site, located in the region that is now Iraq, reveals the traces of one of the oldest known civilizations, notable for its imposing ziggurat and the famous Royal Tombs.

Ur: Where Legends Take Shape in Clay Bricks

Ur, located on the banks of the Euphrates, was a flourishing Sumerian city in ancient times. Its advanced architecture, the creation of legal codes and the connection with the epic of Gilgamesh consolidate it as a crucial cultural and religious center in the history of Mesopotamian civilization.

Sir Leonard Woolley and the Resurrection of Ur

In the 19th century, Sir Leonard Woolley led excavations that rescued the ruins of Ur. Over decades of work, he uncovered strata spanning different historical periods, from the reign of Ur-Nammu to the fall of the dynasty of Isin-Larsa, providing a Complete overview of the city's history.

Ur Resurges: The Sumerian Legacy Revealed

The discovery of Ur in the 19th century was fundamental to understanding the Sumerian civilization and its contribution to humanity. The excavations revealed architectural treasures such as the Ziggurat of Ur and the Royal Tombs, revealing religious aspects, funerary practices and the complexity of life in ancient Mesopotamia.

Legends of Ur: Between Reality and Epic

Although Ur itself is not directly linked to specific myths, Sumerian epics such as that of Gilgamesh provide mythological context to the region. Challenges in interpreting religious inscriptions and rituals add layers of mystery to the understanding of life at Ur.

Between the Sands of Time: Five Fascinating Curiosities

1. The Ziggurat of Ur: A monumental structure that served as a temple and symbol of connection between the earth and the gods.

2. Royal Tombs of Ur: Discoveries of treasures and Queen Puabi, evidencing elaborate funerary practices.

3. Ur-Nammu Stele: Monument with the oldest known legal code, attributed to King Ur-Nammu.

4. The Standard of Ur: Artifact that represents scenes of war and peace, providing information about daily life.

5. Cuneiform Tablets: Thousands of tablets containing inscriptions in cuneiform writing, a vital source of

historical knowledge.

NINEVEH (IRAQ - 19TH CENTURY)

Nineveh, the ancient Assyrian capital of grandeur and power, was unearthed in the 19th century by British archaeologist Austen Henry Layard. This archaeological site, located near modern-day Mosul, Iraq, reveals the vestiges of a militarily formidable civilization that left an indelible mark on the history of Mesopotamia.

Nineveh: Where the Palaces Housed Assyrian Power

Nineveh, founded by Assyrian King Sennacherib, was the jewel of ancient Assyria. Its imposing walls, palaces and the Library of Asurbanipal attest to the splendor and political, military and cultural influence of this city in the region.

Austen Henry Layard and the Reconstruction of Nineveh

In the 19th century, Austen Henry Layard carried out excavations that revealed the wonders of Nineveh. He discovered the Palace of Sennacherib and the Library of Ashurbanipal, unearthing the winged sculptures and cuneiform tablets that provided a unique insight into Assyrian life.

Nineveh Recovered: Testimony of Assyrian Greatness

The discovery of Nineveh in the 19th century was essential to understanding the Assyrian civilization, known for its advanced military organization and contributions to cuneiform writing. The sculptures, inscriptions and reliefs discovered shed light on Assyrian government, religion and culture.

Battles Carved in Stone: Nineveh and its Epics

Although Nineveh itself is not linked to specific myths, Assyrian reliefs recount victories in battle and military cruelty. Challenges in interpreting the inscriptions and understanding Assyrian ideology add layers of complexity to the history of Nineveh.

Among the Palatial Ruins: Five Fascinating Curiosities

1. Palace of Sennacherib: Royal residence with reliefs that illustrate scenes of military conquests and everyday scenes.

2. Library of Ashurbanipal: It housed thousands of cuneiform tablets, including the epic of Gilgamesh and medical texts.

3. The Winged Reliefs: Sculptures that represent winged mythological beings, symbolizing divine protection.

4. The Gates of Nineveh: Entrances decorated with reliefs and sculptures that narrate military triumphs and religious events.

5. Nineveh Canal: Hydraulic engineering that ensured the city's water supply, demonstrating advanced urban planning.

HATTUSA (TÜRKIYE - 19TH CENTURY)

Hattusa, the capital of the mysterious Hittite Empire, was rescued from the shadows of history in the 19th century by French archaeologist Hugo Winckler. This archaeological site, located in the central region of Turkey, reveals the traces of a lost civilization that rivaled the great powers of antiquity.

Hattusa: Where Stones Keep Hittite Secrets

Hattusa, the capital of the Hittite Empire, flourished between the 17th and 12th centuries BC. Its fortified walls, temples and palace complexes bear witness to the splendor of a civilization that challenged Egypt and Babylon at its peak.

Hugo Winckler and the Resurrection of Hattusa

In the 19th century, Hugo Winckler carried out excavations that revealed the wonders of Hattusa. He discovered the Lion Gate and thousands of clay tablets with Hittite cuneiform writing, unearthing the city that defied conventional historical narratives.

Emerging Hattusa: The Forgotten Jewel of Anatolia

The discovery of Hattusa in the 19th century was essential to understanding the Hittite civilization and its role on the ancient international stage. Cuneiform inscriptions, palatial structures, and unearthed artifacts provided detailed insight into Hittite administration, religion, and daily life.

Mythology among the Ruins: Hattusa and her Enigmas

Although Hattusa itself is not directly linked to specific myths, Hittite inscriptions mention deities and mythological events. Challenges in translating the cuneiform tablets and understanding the political structure add layers of intrigue to Hattusa's story.

Among the Hittite Ruins: Five Fascinating Curiosities

1. Gate of the Lions: Monumental entrance with sculptures of winged lions, symbols of Hittite strength.

2. Great Temple: Religious center with a unique structure and rituals dedicated to Hittite deities.

3. Cuneiform Tablets: Administrative records, treaties and myths written in cuneiform writing.

4. Fortified Walls: Defensive system that surrounds the city, highlighting the strategic importance of Hattusa.

5. Lower City and Upper City: Distinction between daily life and palatial areas, evidencing urban planning.

ANCIENT TROY (TÜRKIYE - 19TH CENTURY)

Ancient Troy, the legendary city immortalized in Homer's Iliad, was unearthed in the 19th century by German archaeologist Heinrich Schliemann. This archaeological site, located in what is now Turkey, reveals the strata of a city that witnessed the Trojan War and that endured in the collective memory through the centuries.

Ancient Troy: Between Epic and Reality

Ancient Troy, with its history intertwined with Greek mythology, was an important enclave in ancient times. Its different archaeological layers reflect multiple settlements ranging from the Bronze Age to the Roman era, highlighting its strategic position in the region.

Heinrich Schliemann and the Search for Troy

In the 19th century, Heinrich Schliemann undertook the excavation of Troy with the intention of finding the Homeric city described by Homer. Although his approach was sometimes controversial, he managed to unearth the ruins of an ancient city, identifying Troy as a real place and not just a myth.

Troy Rises: A Link Between Literature and History

The discovery of Ancient Troy in the 19th century was fundamental to reconciling reality with mythology. Through the archaeological layers, the evolution of the city and its connection with the epic events narrated by Homer could be traced, consolidating the historical existence of Troy.

Myths in the Land of Troy: Fact and Legend

The discovery of Troy revitalized the myths of the Iliad. Although no direct evidence of the Homeric heroes was found, the excavations gave rise to new interpretations of the Trojan War. Challenges in the precise correlation between archaeological finds and mythological accounts persist, adding complexity to the legacy of Troy.

Among the Trojan Ruins: Five Fascinating Curiosities

1. Gate of the Lions: Monumental entrance to the fortified city, with sculpted lions as guardians.

2. Walls of Troy VI: Vestiges of the fortifications of Troy VI, associated with the possible Trojan War.

3. Priam's Treasure: Finds of gold and jewels, linked by Schliemann to Priam, king of Troy.

4. Teatro de Troya: Amphitheater that suggests the presence of cultural and artistic activities in the city.

5. Troy in Later Literature: The influence of Troy on literary and artistic works throughout the centuries.

URARTU (ARMENIA - 19TH CENTURY)

Urartu, the enigmatic kingdom of the Iron Age, was unearthed in the 19th century by explorers and archaeologists who ventured into the lands of Armenia. This kingdom, known for its advanced fortified architecture and mysterious cuneiform inscriptions, rises from the shadows of the past to reveal a unique culture.

Urartu: Fortresses in the Summits of Armenia

Urartu, also known as the Kingdom of Van, flourished between the 9th and 6th centuries BC. in the Armenian highlands. Its strategically built fortresses and complex hydraulic systems reflect an advanced society that challenged the great powers of the region.

First Encounters with Urartu

Throughout the 19th century, explorers and archaeologists, such as Friedrich Eduard Schulz and Hormuzd Rassam, ventured into Armenian lands and discovered the ruins of Urartu. They found cuneiform inscriptions, fortresses, temples and a network of irrigation canals, revealing a culture that until then was little known.

Urartu Revealed: An Iron Age Enigma

The discovery of Urartu in the 19th century was crucial to understanding a civilization that has left few traces in historical sources. Cuneiform inscriptions revealed aspects of Urartian religion, administration and language, while strategic fortresses indicated a militarily advanced society.

Urartian Mythology: Between Reality and Legend

Urartu's lack of direct literary and mythological sources poses challenges to understanding its beliefs and myths. However, inscriptions and artifacts provide clues to deities and rituals, inviting speculation about the Urartian pantheon.

Among the Ruins of the Iron Age: Five Fascinating Curiosities

1. Erebuni Fortress: Fortified city that served as an administrative and military center.

2. Irrigation Canals: Complex hydraulic systems that demonstrate the advanced engineering of Urartu.

3. Cuneiform Inscriptions: Documents written in the Urartian language that provide information about culture and administration.

4. Temples and Altars: Places of worship that suggest specific religious practices.

5. Cultural Influence: Traces of Urartian influence in the region, from architecture to agricultural practices.

MACHU PICCHU (PERU - 1911)

Machu Picchu, the architectural jewel of the Incas, was revealed to the world in 1911 by the American explorer and archaeologist Hiram Bingham. This archaeological site, nestled in the Peruvian Andes, stands as an impressive testimony of the engineering, culture and spirituality of the Inca civilization.

Machu Picchu: City in the Clouds of the Incas

Machu Picchu, located more than 2,400 meters above sea level, is an extraordinarily well-preserved Inca city. With its agricultural terraces, temples, and astronomical structures, it represents the height of Inca art and urban planning, possibly serving as a retreat for Emperor Pachacutec.

Hiram Bingham and the Discovery of Machu Picchu

In 1911, Hiram Bingham, in search of the lost city of Vilcabamba, arrived at Machu Picchu by chance. Marveled by the magnificence of the site, Bingham dedicated his efforts to its exploration and study. Their excavations and studies revealed details about Inca architecture, agriculture and astronomy.

Machu Picchu Resurges: Treasure of the Incas Revealed

The discovery of Machu Picchu in 1911 was transcendental for the understanding of the Inca civilization. The city, hidden for centuries, provided valuable information about daily life, religious practices and sophisticated Inca architecture. Its relative isolation contributed to its astonishing state of preservation.

The Charm of Machu Picchu: Between History and Legend

Although Machu Picchu itself is not shrouded in specific myths, its location and architecture suggest cosmological and spiritual meanings to the Incas. Challenges in interpreting the exact functions of the structures and their connection to the Inca worldview persist, adding an aura of mystery.

In the Heart of the Andes: Five Fascinating Curiosities

1. Intihuatana: The carved stone that served as a sundial and focal point in religious ceremonies.

2. Agricultural Terraces: Ingenious terrace farming systems that demonstrated the skill of the Incas in water management.

3. Temple of the Sun: Structure dedicated to solar deities, with windows strategically positioned for astronomical events.

4. Inca Trails: Network of roads that connected Machu Picchu with other important sites of the empire.

5. Strategic Isolation: The remote location of Machu Picchu

at the top of the Andes, possibly to preserve its sacredness.

MOHENJO-DARO (PAKISTAN - 1922)

Mohenjo-daro, the jewel of the ancient Indus Valley civilization, was rediscovered in 1922 by British archaeologist Sir John Marshall. This archaeological site, located in modern-day Pakistan, reveals the traces of a city planned with advanced urban techniques and health systems, testimony to the sophistication of the Indus Valley civilization.

Mohenjo-daro: City of the Indus Valley

Mohenjo-daro, which flourished between 2600 and 1900 BC, represents one of the most advanced urban centers of its time. With its straight streets, drainage systems and planned architecture, it reveals the social organization and technological ingenuity of the ancient Indus Valley civilization.

Sir John Marshall and the Resurrection of Mohenjo-daro

In 1922, Sir John Marshall led the excavations that uncovered the ruins of Mohenjo-daro. Urban planning, public baths, and residential structures revealed an advanced civilization in which art, writing, and technology coexisted in harmony.

Mohenjo-daro Revealed: An Enigma of the Indus Valley

The discovery of Mohenjo-daro in 1922 was essential to understanding the Indus Valley civilization, a mysterious culture with no deciphered writing. Evidence of trade, sophisticated artifacts and advanced drainage systems underline the complexity of this ancient society.

The Silence of Mohenjo-daro: Among Undeciphered Scriptures

Mohenjo-daro lacks direct literary and mythological texts, which poses challenges in interpreting its beliefs and myths. Seals and objects found with undeciphered inscriptions add an air of mystery to the Indus Valley culture.

In the Traces of the Indus Valley Civilization: Five Fascinating Curiosities

1. Public Toilets: Complex drainage systems connected to public toilets, indicating a concern for hygiene.

2. The Great Bath: A rectangular pool that raises questions about its ritual or ceremonial use.

3. Indus Writing: Symbols and seals that constitute a writing not yet deciphered, challenging archaeologists.

4. Terracotta Figurines: Figures representing everyday life, animals and deities, demonstrating advanced artistic skills.

5. Planned City: Straight streets and a sewer network suggest careful urban planning.

MONTE ALBÁN (MEXICO - 1931)

Monte Albán, the ancient Zapotec city rising above the mountains of Oaxaca, was excavated and explored in 1931 by Mexican archaeologist Alfonso Caso. This archaeological site, dating from the preclassic to the postclassic Mesoamerican period, reveals the greatness of a culture that managed to integrate architecture with the landscape in a unique way.

Monte Albán: City in the Heights of Oaxaca

Monte Albán, which flourished from approximately 500 BC. until 800 AD, stands out for its strategic location on a high plateau. With its imposing pyramids, plazas and astronomical observatories, the Zapotec city shows a harmony between architecture and mountainous topography.

Alfonso Caso and the Discovery of Monte Albán

In 1931, Alfonso Caso led excavations that unearthed the secrets of Monte Albán. He discovered tombs, monuments and complex urban structures that attest to the cultural development and artistic sophistication of the Zapotec civilization.

Monte Albán Resurges: Cradle of the Zapotec Civilization

The discovery of Monte Albán in 1931 was vital to understanding the Zapotec culture and its role in the Mesoamerican panorama. The sculptures, ceramics and architecture reveal a cultural flourishing that integrated the Olmec and Mixtec influence, leaving a legacy written in stone.

Monte Albán in the Mesoamerican Mosaic: Between the Real and the Mythical

Although there are no specific myths associated with Monte Albán, inscriptions and artistic representations offer clues about rituals, deities, and the city's connection to Zapotec cosmogony. Challenges in accurately interpreting these inscriptions add layers of mystery.

Among the Carved Stones of Oaxaca: Five Fascinating Curiosities

1. Ball Game: A ball game field, indicating the importance of this ritual sport in Mesoamerican culture.

2. Underground Tombs: Discovery of tombs rich in funerary offerings, evidencing beliefs in life after death.

3. Building J (Dancers Building): Famous for its slabs with stylized human figures, interpreted as prisoners or dancers.

4. Observatory: Structures that suggest astronomical observations and the integration of the calendar in urban planning.

5. Plaza de los Danzantes: A ceremonial space with carved

slabs, enigmatic and full of symbolism, which still baffle researchers.

LASCAUX CAVE (FRANCE - 1940)

Lascaux Cave, a treasure trove of prehistoric rock art, was discovered in 1940 by four French teenagers. This archaeological site, located in the Dordogne region, illustrates the artistic skill and life of Upper Paleolithic communities, offering a unique window into prehistory.

Lascaux Cave: A Sanctuary of Paleolithic Art

The Lascaux Cave, with its walls decorated with more than 600 paintings and engravings, presents an exceptional insight into the life of Upper Paleolithic hunter-gatherers. Animals, human figures and symbols adorn the walls, capturing the artistic essence and spiritual connection of these ancient communities.

Four Teenagers and an Encounter with History

In 1940, Marcel Ravidat and three friends discovered the Lascaux Cave while exploring the region. Its amazing discovery led to the recognition of this prehistoric sanctuary. The initial discovery was kept secret for a time to prevent damage to the paintings before authorities were notified.

Lascaux Revealed: Window to the Ancient World

The discovery of the Lascaux Cave in 1940 was crucial to understanding the art, culture and beliefs of Paleolithic communities. The paintings, dated to around 15,000 years ago, offer a unique perspective on the worldview of these ancient artists and their relationship with the environment.

Lascaux in Myth: Between the Known and the Unknown

Although Lascaux is not shrouded in specific myths, the lack of complete understanding about the exact purpose of the paintings has given rise to various speculations and theories. The mystery surrounding the choice of animals, location and meaning of the paintings adds an aura of enigma.

Among the Rocks and Paleolithic Colors: Five Fascinating Curiosities

1. Hall of the Bulls: Highlighting the representation of bulls, horses and deer, this hall is the artistic heart of Lascaux.

2. Sophisticated Painting Technique: Details and shadows that suggest the use of advanced techniques for the time, such as pigment blowing.

3. Wounded Man: Human figure with a spear stuck in it, whose interpretation still sparks debates about its meaning.

4. Feline Camera: Detailed representations of felines that show the artists' ability to capture movements and

expressions.

5. Lascaux IV Replica: The reproduction of the cave, Lascaux IV, allows visitors to experience the paintings without damaging the original site.

QUMRAN CAVES (WEST BANK - 1947)

The Qumran Caves, famous for housing the Dead Sea Scrolls, were discovered in 1947 by a young Bedouin in the West Bank region. This archaeological find, which covers biblical texts and sectarian writings, sheds light on the life and beliefs of a Jewish community in ancient times.

Qumran Caves: Sanctuary of the Dead Sea Scrolls

Located near the Dead Sea, the Qumran Caves have revealed a unique collection of ancient manuscripts. These texts, which include fragments of almost all the books of the Old Testament as well as sectarian writings, are a window into the beliefs and practices of a Jewish community in the second centuries BC. - I AD

The Bedouin and the Forgotten Scrolls

In 1947, a young Bedouin, while chasing a lost goat, threw a stone into a cave near the Dead Sea and heard the sound of something breaking. Inside he found vases with ancient manuscripts. This chance discovery marked the beginning of systematic exploration of the Qumran Caves.

Dead Sea Scrolls: Link to the Biblical Past

The discovery of the Dead Sea Scrolls in the Qumran Caves has been vital to understanding the transmission and preservation of biblical texts. In addition to the canonical texts, the sectarian scrolls offer a unique insight into the beliefs and practices of a sectarian Jewish community that lived during the Second Temple period.

The Scrolls and Historical Speculations

Although there are no specific myths or legends associated with the Qumran Caves, the precise identification of the community that produced the scrolls and their connection to historical events, such as the destruction of the Second Temple, remains a matter of debate. Speculation about the connection to the Essenes adds layers of mystery.

In the Footprints of the Scrolls: Five Fascinating Curiosities

1. Sectarian Scrolls: Texts that reveal the beliefs and rules of a separatist community, possibly the Essenes.

2. Biblical Scrolls: They include fragments of almost all the books of the Old Testament, some in Hebrew and others in Aramaic.

3. Genizah of Qumran: The repository of discarded or deteriorated manuscripts, evidence of a careful process of copying and selection.

4. Great Cave Four: Where most of the scrolls were found, suggesting a significant place for the community.

5. Theological Implications: The Dead Sea Scrolls have influenced the understanding of the textual transmission

of Scripture and theological discussions.

CATALHÖYÜK (TÜRKIYE - 1958)

Catalhöyük, an ancient Neolithic city that prospered between 7500 and 5700 BC, was discovered and excavated in 1958 by British archaeologist James Mellaart. This archaeological site, located on the Anatolian plateau, reveals a complex society and the first evidence of urban life in human history.

Catalhöyük: Neolithic City without Streets

Catalhöyük is an archaeological wonder that defies conventional urban norms. With its terraced houses and absence of streets, it suggests a unique communal way of life in which social interconnectedness and agriculture were fundamental to survival.

James Mellaart and the Resurgence of Catalhöyük

In 1958, James Mellaart began excavations at Catalhöyük, revealing a complex overlap of dwellings, evidence of several phases of occupation. The finds, which include wall paintings, tools and artefacts, paint a detailed portrait of life in the Neolithic.

Catalhöyük Unearthed: Neolithic in Perspective

The discovery of Catalhöyük in 1958 was crucial to understanding the transition from hunter-gatherer communities to agricultural and urban societies. The lack of streets and the close proximity of homes suggest a cooperative social structure, while the wall paintings reflect rich artistic expression.

Catalhöyük in Imagination and Reality

Although there are no specific myths associated with Catalhöyük, wall paintings depicting anthropomorphic figures and ritual scenes have led to speculation about myths and beliefs of the community. The precise interpretation of these images remains the subject of study.

Exploring Neolithic Singularities: Five Fascinating Curiosities

1. Mural Paintings: Representations of human figures, animals and ritual scenes that offer a unique vision of the Neolithic worldview.

2. Homes without Streets: The tight arrangement of homes without a street layout, suggesting a communal and compact way of life.

3. Burials under Houses: Practice of burying the dead under houses, indicating a deep connection with the community and the house.

4. Textile Art: Evidence of elaborate textile techniques, highlighting the importance of textile production in Catalhöyük society.

5. Ritualistic Pergolas: Pergola-like structures associated

with rituals and ceremonies, revealing distinctive cultural practices.

POSSIBLE (SYRIA - 1964)

The ancient city of Ebla, whose remains are found in present-day northern Syria, was rediscovered and excavated in 1964 by the Italian archaeologist Paolo Matthiae. This archaeological site, which flourished during the third millennium BC, revealed a thriving civilization with a rich cultural heritage and a cuneiform writing system that transformed our understanding of ancient history.

Ebla: City of Cuneiform Archives

Ebla, known for its extensive cuneiform archives, was a highly developed city-state that prospered between 2500 and 2250 BC. With an economy based on trade and advanced administration, Ebla left a significant mark on the ancient history of Mesopotamia.

Paolo Matthiae y el Renacimiento de Ebla

In 1964, Paolo Matthiae began excavations at Tell Mardikh, the site of ancient Ebla. Cuneiform clay tablets containing administrative records, literature, and correspondence were soon discovered, revealing the existence of a prosperous and sophisticated city.

Ebla and its Impact on Ancient History

The discovery of Ebla in 1964 was revolutionary, as the cuneiform tablets found provided detailed information about the politics, economy and culture of the city. Ebla became a key center in the region's trade and its written records transformed the understanding of the Akkadian language and history of the third millennium BC.

Ebla in the Cultural Mosaic of Mesopotamia

Although there are no specific myths associated with Ebla, the tablets have revealed information about diplomatic relations and religious rituals. Accurately identifying Ebla's location in the historical narrative has also been a constant challenge.

Exploring the City of Tablets: Five Fascinating Curiosities

1. Royal Archives: Tablets containing administrative records and correspondence of the kings, revealing details about government and diplomatic relations.

2. Palace G: The discovery of Palace G, which housed the tablets from the royal archives, marked a milestone in the excavation.

3. Epic Literature: Texts that contain myths and epics, contributing to Mesopotamian literature with stories of heroes and deities.

4. Eblaite Language: The identification of the Eblaite language, which contributed significantly to the understanding of Semitic languages.

5. Transregional Trade: Evidence of trade with cities such as Mari and Sumer, underscoring the economic importance of Ebla in the region.

GÖBEKLI TEPE (TURQUÍA - 1994)

Göbekli Tepe, the oldest known archaeological site of megalithic structures, was discovered in 1994 by German archaeologist Klaus Schmidt in southeastern Turkey. This revolutionary find has redefined our understanding of prehistory, revealing complex ritual structures erected by hunter-gatherer societies long before the emergence of agriculture.

Göbekli Tepe: Temple of the Ancient Ages

Göbekli Tepe is an archaeological complex consisting of enormous stone pillars, sculpted and decorated with animal reliefs, dating back to approximately 9600 BC. This prehistoric temple challenges previous perceptions by demonstrating the ability of ancient societies to build monumental structures.

Klaus Schmidt and the Revelation of Göbekli Tepe

In 1994, during an archaeological survey in the region, Klaus Schmidt identified earthen mounds hiding carved stone pillars. This initial discovery led to intensive excavations, revealing the magnitude and age of Göbekli Tepe.

Göbekli Tepe and the Enigma of Prehistory

The discovery of Göbekli Tepe in 1994 transformed the narrative of prehistory. Megalithic structures, created by hunter-gatherers, challenge previous conceptions about the constructive capacity of pre-agrarian societies. This archaeological site is fundamental to understanding cultural and ritual development in the early stages of human civilization.

Göbekli Tepe between Mystery and Interpretation

Although there are no specific myths associated with Göbekli Tepe, the exact purpose of these ritual structures remains a subject of speculation. The absence of nearby settlements suggests that this site may have been a place of pilgrimage, rituals or even astronomical events.

Exploring the Prehistoric Temple: Five Fascinating Curiosities

1. Decorated Pillars: The carved pillars display reliefs of animals, including sculptures of lions, foxes and birds, representing impressive artistic skill.

2. Architectural Complexity: The structures, some with cantilevered stone roofs, indicate advanced planning and construction for the time.

3. Absence of Dwellings: Unlike other prehistoric sites, Göbekli Tepe lacks evidence of permanent dwellings, intensifying the mystery about its purpose.

4. T Stelae in the Core: Some of the structures present T-shaped central pillars, suggesting possible symbolic

connotations.

5. Astronomical Importance: Some researchers suggest that the orientation of the structures could be related to astronomical events, marking stellar cycles.

KARNAK TEMPLE (EGYPT - ANCIENT)

The Temple of Karnak, a monumental complex in the ancient city of Thebes, is one of the most impressive architectural achievements of Egyptian civilization. Its construction took place over several centuries and spanned multiple dynasties. This temple, dedicated primarily to the god Amun-Ra, stands as an imposing testimony to the greatness and spirituality of ancient Egypt.

Karnak Temple: City of the Gods

The Karnak Temple is a vast complex of temples, shrines and processional avenues. Its construction spanned from the Middle Kingdom to the Ptolemaic period, being the main religious center dedicated to Amun-Ra, the main deity of the Egyptian pantheon.

Karnak Through the Centuries

Construction of the Temple of Karnak began in the Middle Kingdom, around 2055 BC, and continued for more than 1,300 years. Its expansion and enrichment took place throughout the Egyptian dynasties, making it a living testimony of the evolution of Egyptian art and architecture.

Karnak as a Spiritual and Cultural Center

The Karnak Temple was not only a place of worship, but also a cultural and administrative center. It hosted religious festivals, rituals and celebrations, and its architectural complexity reflected the importance of Amun-Ra in Egyptian life. Karnak symbolized the connection between the pharaohs and the gods.

The Myth of Karnak and its Modern Challenges

Although there are no specific myths associated with Karnak, the rich iconography carved into reliefs shows scenes of worship, battles and ritual processions. The precise interpretation of these reliefs remains an archaeological and Egyptological challenge.

Exploring the Sacred City: Five Fascinating Curiosities

1. Avenue of Sphinxes: A processional avenue flanked by sphinxes connected Karnak with the Luxor Temple, highlighting the sacred connection between the two.

2. Hypostyle Room: A room with enormous columns, some reaching 21 meters in height, which created an impressive forest of pillars.

3. Monumental Obelisks: Karnak was home to obelisks, some of which were moved to places like Rome and Paris in more recent times.

4. Opet Festival: An important annual religious festival that involved processions and sacred rituals in honor of Amun-Ra.

5. Ongoing Restoration: Over the years, Karnak Temple has been the subject of restoration efforts to preserve its splendor for future generations.

STONEHENGE (UNITED KINGDOM - ANCIENT)

Stonehenge, an iconic megalithic monument on the Salisbury Plains, England, has baffled researchers and visitors for millennia. Built in several phases between the Neolithic and the Bronze Age, Stonehenge is an archaeological enigma that has endured as a symbol of the technical prowess and spirituality of ancient British cultures.

Stonehenge: Circle of Monoliths on the Salisbury Plains

Stonehenge is made up of large monoliths arranged in concentric circles and astronomical alignments. Its construction was carried out in phases between 3000 BC. and 1600 B.C. and has been a site of speculation about its purpose, from an astronomical observatory to a ritual and funerary site.

Construction Phases Over the Millennia

Construction of Stonehenge began in the Neolithic with a circular bench and moat. Later, megalithic stones were erected, some transported from significant distances. Its evolution reflects changes in the society and culture of the time, as well as technological advances in the mobilization of large stones.

Stonehenge as an Observatory and Sacred Place

Stonehenge has been interpreted in various ways, from an astronomical observatory used to track the movement of the sun and moon, to a place of rituals and ceremonies linked to life, death and spirituality. Its alignment with key astronomical events underscores its deep meaning.

Stonehenge in Ancient and Modern Narratives

Although there are no specific myths associated with Stonehenge, local legends have contributed to its mystical aura. Modern challenges include debates about its original purpose and the precise techniques used for its construction, which spark curiosity and speculation.

Exploring the Enigma in Stone: Five Fascinating Curiosities

1. Blue Stones: Some stones, known as blue stones, were transported from Wales, more than 200 kilometers away.

2. Solar Alignment: Stonehenge is aligned with solar events, such as the summer solstice, suggesting advanced knowledge of astronomy.

3. Heelstone: A stone at a certain distance known as a Heelstone acts as a marker for the solstice.

4. Ancient Burials: Burials have been discovered in and around Stonehenge, indicating their role in funerary and spiritual rituals.

5. Stone Moving: Modern theories suggest that the stones were transported using sleds and rollers, but the exact process remains the subject of research.

VALLEY OF THE KINGS (EGYPT - ANCIENT)

The Valley of the Kings, located on the west bank of the Nile River near Luxor, Egypt, is a necropolis containing pharaonic tombs from the 18th to the 20th Dynasty. This archaeological site, known for its richly decorated tombs and exceptional discoveries, represents a unique contribution to our understanding of life after death in ancient Egypt.

Valley of the Kings: Eternal Rest of Pharaohs

The Valley of the Kings served as a burial place for pharaohs and nobles from the 18th to 20th Dynasty, including Tutankhamun and Ramses II. The tombs, carved into the rock, are decorated with hieroglyphics and wall paintings that illustrate the journey of the deceased towards life after death.

The Royal Necropolis Throughout the Dynasties

The construction of tombs in the Valley of the Kings began in the reign of Thutmose I and continued for more than 500 years. Each tomb was designed with intricate passageways and burial chambers, reflecting the Egyptian belief in life after death and the importance of preserving the body.

Funerary Rites and the Egyptian Afterlife

The Valley of the Kings represents an exceptional testimony to the beliefs and funerary rituals of ancient Egypt. Tombs were sacred places where offerings were placed and ceremonies were performed to ensure a successful journey to the afterlife. The reliefs and hieroglyphics provide a unique window into Egyptian cosmology.

The Mythical Narrative of the Royal Tombs

Although there are no specific myths associated with the Valley of the Kings, hieroglyphic inscriptions on the tombs tell the story of the deceased's life, his exploits, and his journey to the underworld. Modern challenges include the conservation of the paintings and the complete understanding of the symbology present in the tombs.

Exploring Eternal Rest: Five Fascinating Curiosities

1. Discovery of Tutankhamun: Tutankhamun's tomb, discovered by Howard Carter in 1922, contained priceless treasures and opened a unique window to the past.

2. Hieroglyphics and Wall Paintings: The tombs are adorned with scenes from the life of the deceased and funerary rituals, providing a detailed visual record.

3. Tomb of Ramses II: Although Ramses II is not buried in the Valley of the Kings, some of his sons and descendants

were found there.

4. Number of Tombs: More than 60 tombs have been identified in the Valley of the Kings, each with its own history and meaning.

5. Conservation and Tourism: Tourism management and tomb conservation are ongoing challenges to preserving this unique heritage.